SOUTHERN STEAM on shed

SOUTHERN
STEAM ON SHED

TONY FAIRCLOUGH AND **ALAN WILLS**

D. BRADFORD BARTON LIMITED

Frontispiece: A rebuilt light Pacific outside Nine Elms shed on 21 September 1965. No. 34090 was selected by the Southern Region to commemorate its own predecessor, the Southern Railway, naming the engine *Sir Eustace Missenden, Southern Railway* after the last Chairman of the Company.

[N. E. Preedy]

© Copyright D. Bradford Barton Ltd ISBN 085153 189X

Published by Enterprise Transport Books Ltd
3 Barnsway, Kings Langley, Hertfordshire WD4 9PW

Printed and bound in Great Britain by BPC Hazell Books Ltd

introduction

The Shed—home of the steam locomotive and, to the railway enthusiast, hallowed ground whose sanctity was enhanced by its inaccessibility. 'No Admittance Except On Business' was the general rule and this gave an air of mystery to the rites which were performed inside the lofty buildings and smoky yards of a locomotive depot. Yet for the professional railwayman there was little of this romanticism about his working life. Hard and unremitting toil in gloomy, draughty and dirty conditions was his lot, yet most men—some serving upwards of fifty years in the Railway service, often at the same depot—guarded the reputation of their shed with a fierce loyalty and looked down on all other establishments as inferior places, not to be compared with their own.

A large Locomotive Running Shed, later renamed Motive Power Depot, was a complex organisation, housing numerous locomotives and employing many men. In command overall was the Shed Master, the Boss who, in modern times was an engineer, while below him were the departmental heads. The Chief Clerk supervised the administration of the depot, which involved a great deal of paper work. The Mechanical Foreman and his staff of fitters, boiler-smiths, washout staff, etc., ensured that the engines were maintained in good working order. Then there were the three Running Foremen, promoted drivers who had the vital task of supervising the footplate crews, ensuring that suitable engines were rostered for each duty and that these left the shed yard in good time to perform their work. These men were usually great 'characters', upon whom depended much of the efficiency and sound working of the shed. Finally there were the enginemen themselves, the drivers and firemen who felt that they were the kings of the railway world. A shed with sixty-odd locomotives would have about 150 pairs of men to work the duties diagrammed to the depot. These men would be divided into Links, or 'gangs' of varying numbers, usually between twelve and twenty in a link. The men worked the rosters in the link, turn and turn about, on a weekly or daily basis. The young men, newly appointed to their grade, spent their first years in preparation and disposal work within the confines of the depot and the surrounding lines and would only occasionally have the chance for a run out on the road. However, on the Southern there was always a shortage of crews at the peak holiday periods so these men were often called upon for a running job. But promotion up the Links would come, first to the Local Goods and then the Heavy Goods Links and later to the Mixed Traffic and Passenger Links. Usually around No.3 Link was the 'Spare Gang', a group of men with considerable experience and a wide route knowledge who could take over any duty in the event of sickness or holidays as well as being available to work special trains of any class over the lines in their district. Pride of place went, of course, to the No.1 Link, the 'Top Link' or 'Main Line Gang', which usually worked the best express duties allocated to the shed. Men were in their mid-fifties before they reached this link and therefore had a wealth of experience and skill behind them when tackling the prestige turns of the depot. For some men, though, misfortune could come in the form of ill-health or eyesight failure, when work would be found for them on shunting and station pilot turns.

It is the intention in this volume to present a collection of shed scenes, taken mostly in the post-war years, at a variety of sheds throughout the Southern Region. About half of the Region's sheds are included and a further selection will appear in a second volume later. The editors hope that these scenes will provide the reader with a visual reminder of those days when steam engines were to be seen in great numbers at many locations throughout the South and West of England. The record companies can now supply the nostalgic sounds of steam engines at work, but one memory is difficult to revive—the *smell* of a locomotive depot, that wonderfully sour mixture of steam and warm oil, sulphurous smoke and ashes, water and hot metal that somehow was an engine shed. This will have to be left to the imagination.

Bulleid Pacific No. 34046 *Braunton* pays Nine Elms shed a visit before returning home to Bou mouth later in the day. The engine is running on the through road into the shed yard towards turntable; engines requiring a longer stay on the pits, such as No. 34062 *17 Squadron* queue the line in the background. [N.E. Pre

A selection of motive power on show at Nine Elms in June 1959. Although the railway had been nationalised for over eleven years, all the engines visible are pre-war types, ranging from 'Schools' No. 30904 *Lancing* on the extreme left, past a pair of 'L1' 4-4-0s Nos. 31788 and 31789, 'U' Class 2-6-0 No. 31624 and two 'E1s' on the right. These various 4-4-0s were recent arrivals from the Eastern Section, having been displaced from their old haunts by the spread of the electrified system down towards the Kent coast resorts.

[Peter Winding]

9

With the large coaling tower dominating the skyline in the background, 'West Country' Pacific No. 34019 *Bideford* stands with steam up outside Nine Elms 'new shed' on 9 November 1964. In its heyday this depot had a considerable allocation of light Pacifics, having 14 in 1953. These were used for express work from Waterloo to Exeter, Southampton, Bournemouth and Weymouth.

[A. R. Butcher]

A cross section of locomotive types on shed in June 1959. No. 35018 *British India Line* was one of Nine Elms' 11 'Merchant Navy' 4-6-2s which were used on the hardest turns to Exeter and Weymouth. Urie 'S15' 4-6-0 No. 30511, of nearby Feltham shed, will probably work a heavy freight from Nine Elms goods yard down to Southampton, while 'M7' 0-4-4T No. 30241 will be engaged in carriage shunting work at Waterloo.   [Peter Winding]

Standard Class '5' 4-6-0 No. 73115, followed by No. 35020 *Bibby Line*, comes off the pits towards the turntable, June 1959. [Peter Winding]

Rebuilt 'Merchant Navy' No. 35011 *General Steam Navigation,* of Bournemouth shed, pauses under the chute of the coal hopper on its way out of the depot after turning and engine requirements, 12 May 1963. Pacifics working up from Bournemouth, 108 miles away, did not usually require additional coal in London, but if the up trip had been a hard one the crew might take on some extra fuel for the run home.

[D. M. Cox]

Bulleid's first locomotive, albeit in rebuilt form, No. 35001 *Channel Packet*, stands over the ash pits at Nine Elms, October 1964. Cleaning locomotive fires after a long run was one of the most unpleasant jobs the railway had to offer, while the piles of clinker and ash had often to be hand-loaded into wagons for disposal. It was this sort of labour which spelt doom for steam traction in Britain.

[A. R. Butcher]

This row of engines at Nine Elms on 1 April 1958 shows only one Standard, No. 73116, among a variety of SR types.   [A. R. Butcher]

By 17 July, six years later, Standards predominate, with only one SR locomotive, a 'Q' Class 0-6-0, on view.
    [P. H. Groom]

The second batch of 'Merchant Navy' Pacifics, Nos. 21C11-20, went new to Nine Elms in 1944 and remained intact there for several years. This April 1950 photograph of *French Line C.G.T.*, renumbered 35019 by B R, shows the blue livery used at that time for the most powerful passenger engines. Many of the Top Link men at Nine Elms preferred the Pacifics in their original Bulleid condition. For one thing, the enclosed valve gear meant less machinery for the driver to oil before a trip! The senior links of enginemen at Nine Elms worked out-and-home turns to Bournemouth and Salisbury, the 'Spare Gang' worked the boat trains, and mixed traffic men worked heavy freights from Nine Elms yard to Portsmouth, Southampton and Salisbury.   [Peter Winding]

Engines could only reach the 'old shed' at Nine Elms by way of the turntable, which was normally set, as in this view, for the road leading from the pits. The 'new shed', seen through the smoke haze on the right, could be reached without recourse to the table.　[Lens of Sutton]

bury's most famous engine, No. 30453 *King Arthur*, was a frequent visitor to Nine Elms. After being double-manned
vo pairs of Top Link enginemen in the pre-war years, the engine continued to work relief and semi-fast trains to
capital from the West Country until its withdrawal in 1961.   [N. E. Preedy]

'Battle of Britain' 4-6-2 No. 34050 *Royal Observer Corps* turns on the vacuum-operated table, Nine
Elms, July 1963. No doubt the inhabitants of the adjacent flats did not lament the passing of the
steam engine, as the great running shed must have made their homes noisy, smoky places. Today
the site is occupied by the new Covent Garden Market.   [N. E. Preedy]

No. 30493 was one of four large 'G 16' 4-8-0Ts which Robert Urie designed in 1921 for shunting the hump yard at Feltham. The 95-ton engine is seen on a visit to Nine Elms in June 1959.   [Peter Winding]

Brighton-built ex-LBSCR engines were used by Nine Elms for shunting and empty stock working. 'E4' 0-6-2T No. 32563 poses in the yard, in June 1959.
                    [Peter Winding]

Maunsell also designed an eight-coupled tank for heavy shunting work. Eight of these 'Z' Class 0-8-0Ts were built in 1929, being unusual in having three cylinders. No. 30955, seen in May 1951, was used in the extensive goods yard situated close to the shed. Nine Elms also had a number of smaller shunting tanks for use in the numerous yards of south-west London.
[Peter Winding]

The seven 4-6-0s which Maunsell rebuilt in 1934 from the Lawson Billinton Baltic tanks of the LBSCR went to Nine Elms shed for express duties but the Western Section crews found them greatly inferior to their own 'King Arthurs'. Soon they were relegated to slow passenger and milk turns and by 24 September 1955, when this view of No. 32331 *Beattie* was taken, they were working from Basingstoke on semi-fast passenger jobs.

[A. E. Bennett]

Two 0-4-4 tanks outside Nine Elms shed on 14 June 1961. 'H' No.31326 and 'M7' No.30039 were designed by Wainwright and Drummond respectively for passenger work, but as all short distance local services in this area were electrified, these tanks will be occupied with empty stock working in and around Waterloo. Hauling the heavy twelve coach sets to and from Clapham Junction was extremely arduous work for such small machines but they coped well for many years. [D. T. Cobbe]

This pre-war photo, taken by the coal stage, shows the Nine Elms shed pilot, No. 949 *Hecate*, an 0-8-0 tank built by Hawthorn Leslie in 1904 for the Kent & East Sussex Railway. 'King Arthur' 4-6-0 No. 790 *Sir Villiers* was one of Bournemouth's crack Top Link engines of the mid 1930's.

[Peter Winding]

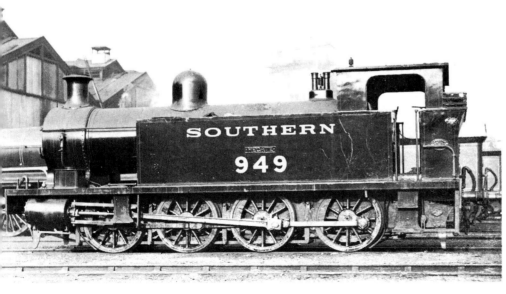

This view of *Hecate*, taken on 10 March 1934, shows the high standards of cleanliness which prevailed in those days. Labour was cheap, so cleaners were plentiful, and indifferent work meant quick dismissal followed by the dole queue. Probably a shed of the size of Nine Elms would have forty to fifty boys to maintain its stud of ninety-odd engines in fine external condition.

[H. C. Casserley]

A last look at Nine Elms shows 'West Country' No.34002 *Salisbury* being prepared for a run to the West on 12 July 1964. The fireman has been cleaning the char from the smokebox, a miserable task made more difficult on the Bulleids by the height of the door above the plating on which the fireman had to stand. The introduction of the self-cleaning smoke box to certain classes was a great boon to the hard-worked men. Incidentally, the work of fire-dropping, etc., was performed by shed labourers on ex-Great Western lines, which made the work of disposal much easier for foot-platemen after a hard run.

[N. E. Preedy]

Basingstoke seemed always to have to use other sheds' cast-offs for its semi-fast passenger turns to Waterloo and Salisbury. No. 30755 *The Red Knight* was at Nine Elms for many years. It was the only Urie 'Arthur' to retain 22in cylinders and, as modified by Bulleid with a Lemaitre blast pipe, proved to be the finest performer of all the Urie 4-6-0s. By 17 April 1957, when seen outside Basingstoke shed, it was the only surviving 'N15' with the large diameter chimney.   [A. R. Butcher]

No. 30455 *Sir Launcelot* spent most of its years at Salisbury before moving to Nine Elms and then, by April 1957, to Basingstoke. This engine still retains the Drummond type tender with inside bearings which was originally fitted to the splendid Nos. 448-457 series when they were built at Eastleigh in 1925.
      [A. R. Butcher]

Southern Railway designs were still much in evidence at Basingstoke as late as 1963. 'S 15' 4-6-0 No. 30840, having worked down a heavy freight from its home at Feltham, is coming on to the shed, while two sister engines wait in the yard. Two Moguls, Standard Class '4' No. 76067 and a Maunsell 'U' Class, are also visible. Basingstoke had extensive yards for marshalling the freight trains which converged on the station from the London area, the West Country, Southampton and from points North via the Western Region at Reading. The proximity of the shed to the busy station can be seen in this view, taken on 31 August.

[A. R. Butcher]

A double-chimney Standard Class '4' 4-6-0, No. 75075, being prepared for duty in the shed yard at Basingstoke. These small but lively 4-6-0s were among the last regular users of the depot. Although the engine carries no shed plate, it was one of the class allocated to Eastleigh at that date (10 September 1966). As the Southern had no water troughs, the men tried to top up the tank as their engine was about to go off the Loco; this particular Standard is coupled to a 4,725 gallon tender.

[A. R. Butcher]

A much earlier design of 4-6-0 at Basingstoke. No. 30333 was nominally a Urie rebuild of one of Drummond's disastrous 'F13' 4-6-0s of 1905, but little of the original engines remained. The boiler shell and the long flat firegrate were retained, and these six locomotives, Nos. 30330-335, forming part of the 'H15' Class, were always difficult to fire. Salisbury men, with their long experience of the class, could make them steam and often used them on heavy freight turns to Basingstoke. In pre-war days they were the longest 4-6-0s which could use the turntable then installed at the depot.

[P. J. Lynch]

Basingstoke was a small three-road shed situated 48 miles from Waterloo. The depot's principal turns were the semi-fasts to Waterloo and Salisbury. 'Lord Nelson' 4-6-0 No.30857 *Lord Howe* is receiving attention close to modern Standard Class '5' No.73089 *Maid of Astolat*. Below, 'King Arthur' No.30765 *Sir Gareth* has taken on its five-ton quota of coal from the stage and, having filled the 5,000 gallon water tank, the driver pulls the hose clear of the tender.   [Peter Winding]

An interesting contrast at Basingstoke: the Farnborough Air Show has brought restored Ivatt 'Large Atlantic' No.251 to the depot for engine requirements, while 'Schools' No.30901 *Winchester* of St. Leonards has worked in a special from the South Coast, 12 September 1954.

[L. Elsey]

This 1928 view shows the S R and G W R sheds at Andover Junction. The Southern shed is on the left and the small engines allocated would work trains off the ex-M S W J line to Southampton, via Stockbridge.

[H. C. Casserley]

The Southern shed at Reading was overshadowed by the large Western establishment close by. The South Eastern Railway penetrated to the Berkshire town by a roundabout route and services were run by the SR to the South Coast via Redhill from Reading (South). This view shows the east end of the shed, with a Standard Class '4' Mogul, No. 76053, raising steam, October 1956.
[Peter Winding]

The shed was close to the running lines, the nearest being the SR route which joins the Western main line at this point. Southern engines working up from the South coast on inter-Regional holiday trains were relieved here by Western engines on some through workings.   [Lens of Sutton]

'S15' 4-6-0s were not common on Reading shed, but No. 30837 is something rather special. As the last surviving Maunsell 4-6-0, it achieved considerable fame in its latter days on enthusiasts' specials and has called at Reading for servicing on 2 May 1965. This fine engine, like its 24 sisters, was a good steamer to the last, as the column of steam from the safety valves discloses.

[D. M. Cox]

Maunsell Moguls were the mainstay of the Reading to Redhill services for many years. In the early 1950's, Reading had an allocation of eight 'U' Class 2-6-0s, which hauled the locals on this hilly cross-country line. One of the last survivors of the class, No. 31809 of Guildford shed, is seen on 6 February 1965. This engine, one of twenty rebuilt from 2-6-4 tanks, is in poor condition, with steam leaking profusely.

[D. M.Cox]

No. 31614 has worked up to Reading from Redhill on 21 June 1955. The 'Us' Nos. 31610-39 differed slightly from the '31790' rebuilds, the most noticeable point being the smaller splashers of the former. Both varieties were equally at home on medium-weight passenger trains on sharply graded routes, hence their lengthy years of service.

[Brian Morrison]

Dorchester shed in 1950;
at this date ten engines
were on its strength,
including one 'U' Class
2-6-0. Gradually,
Weymouth took over
Dorchester's work
in this area.

[L. & G. R. P.]

The small shed at
Winchester houses one
'B4' 0-4-0T, No. 30096, on
6 July 1963.

[H. C. Casserley]

Lymington, 1950; usually
a couple of tanks were
stabled overnight for
working the short
branch to Brockenhurst.
'M7s' were the regular
engines for many years,
giving way to the larger
Standards in the final
years of steam working.

[L. & G. R. P.]

A contrast in light Pacifics at Weymouth, 18 June 1967. Unrebuilt 'West Country' No. 34023 *Blackmore Vale* and rebuilt 'Battle of Britain' No. 34089 *602 Squadron* have both been cleaned for working the RCTS 'Farewell to Steam' tour. The fireman of the 'B.B.' trims his coal forward for the return trip to London as No. 34023 shatters the peace by blowing off at 280lbs per sq.in. The light Pacifics in their original condition had no front ashpan dampers and it was difficult to keep control of the fire when they were standing on shed.

[A. R. Butcher]

Somehow the Bulleids did not seem to be really at home on such a typically Great Western shed as Weymouth; the coal stage and water column have all the hall marks of Swindon about them as 'West Country' No. 34002 *Salisbury* takes on 5,000 gallons of water, 3 July 1966.   [A. R. Butcher]

No. 34089, minus its nameplate *602 Squadron*, turns on the standard G W R type table at Weymouth, 18 June 1967, not many days before steam working ceased on 9 July.

[A. R. Butcher]

Weymouth shed underwent a transformation in the 1960s. Originally a G W R depot with 'Saints' and 'Halls' among its thirty locomotives allocated, it became the rendezvous for Bulleids and B R Standards in its latter days. No. 34024 *Tamar Valley* takes water, 1 April 1967.

[M. J. Messenger]

Pacific smoke deflectors in Weymouth shed, 1 April 1967.

[M. J. Messenger]

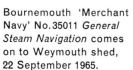

Bournemouth 'Merchant Navy' No. 35011 *General Steam Navigation* comes on to Weymouth shed, 22 September 1965.

[J. R. Besley]

No. 34052 *Lord Dowding*, seen by the south side of the large coal stage on 27 August 1965, was a Salisbury engine for many years. The mechanical coaler was installed during the Second World War to speed up the refuelling of the Bulleid Pacifics which arrived at the depot in 1941. Salisbury always had a number of light Pacifics, having seven in 1953 and twenty in 1963. Salisbury men worked many of the express turns to Waterloo and Exeter, plus a wide variety of duties to Portsmouth, Bournemouth, Eastleigh and Southampton, as well as several turns to Bristol and Cardiff, using ex-GWR engines.

[D. T. Cobbe]

In Southern Railway days, all trains changed engines at Salisbury, which meant that the pits at the shed were exceedingly busy coping with visiting engines and the 80-odd locomotives of Salisbury's own allocation. But from February 1950, through engine workings were instituted between Waterloo and Exeter on a number of trains, eliminating 27 engine changes at Salisbury station. This eased the situation in the shed yard and the number of engines shedded was reduced, settling down to some fifty engines, many of which were express and large mixed-traffic types. Salisbury men continued to work many of the trains, re-manning at the station. Here, Exmouth Junction Pacific No. 35011 *General Steam Navigation* has come on to the pits, 6 September 1959.

[N. E. Preedy]

A fine line-up at Salisbury on 18 April 1964. Standards Nos. 75067 and 73043 of Eastleigh, with No. 73117 *Vivien* of Nine Elms have steam up, as 'Q' Class 0-6-0 No. 30548 of Eastleigh drops back to the table after working the 'Hampshire Venturer Rail Tour'. The shed was a ten-road structure, with the offices and the enginemen's cabin situated at the back of the building.

[A. R. Butcher]

40

4-4-0s were regular
ormers around Salisbury.
0729 was at the shed for
e years, but had moved on
ournemouth by 13 May 1958
n this view was taken.
se useful Drummond
nes, whose performance
so much improved by
's superheating in the
s, worked stopping trains to
rnemouth, Portsmouth and
vil for many years before
finally gave way to the
ern Standard 76XXX 2-6-0s.
nd is No. 30449 *Sir Torre*,
of the famous 'King
urs' which Salisbury men
dled so well for 35 years.

[Brian Morrison]

The shed yard, 13 October 1962. In the background is an 'S15' 4-6-0, a type used by Salisbury for heavy freight and mixed-traffic work.

[A. E. Bennett]

hint of things to come at
alisbury on 13 May 1965. Only
ne steam engine is visible, No.
4086 *219 Squadron*, which has
team up for the trip home to
righton. The 'Hymek' diesel-
ydraulic has worked in off the
Vestern Region. Nos. 1 and 2
ads on the extreme left were
sed for washing out, and Nos.
and 10 on the right were the
epair roads. On Sundays in the
940's, over 100 engines could
e noted on shed; now the
hole site has been cleared.

[J. R. Besley]

No. 73118 ex-*King Leodegrance* stands fully coaled ready for its return home to London with a semi-fast, 28 March 1965.

[A. R. Butcher]

A stranger on shed at Salisbury, 13 May 1958. No. 30584, one of the three Adams radial tanks shedded at Exmouth Junction for use on the Lyme Regis branch, calls in on its way to Eastleigh for shopping. This engine was built as long ago as 1885, yet it survived its visit to Eastleigh and remained in service until the end of 1960. The GWR tender serves as a reminder that a considerable number of Western Region locomotives used Salisbury shed after the ex-GW depot in the city was closed in 1950.

[Brian Morrison]

Steam had only one more week of life on the Southern when this shed view was recorded for posterity on 30 June 1967. It is interesting to note that, although bereft of name and number plates, this Salisbury 'West Country', No. 34100 *Appledore* is still in superb external condition. The depot was able to maintain its engines in fine fettle until the very end, thanks to the numbers of cleaners available and the enthusiasm of the shed management. Lying on the floor can be seen the water cock and hoses which would be connected to the washout plugs on the boilers, a job which had to be done weekly in a hard-water district like Wiltshire. The Bulleids were fitted with water softening gear which allowed 56 days between washouts, a considerable help to the shed staff.

[N. E. Preedy]

Salisbury shed yard, 30 September 1967. The depot was crowded with engines throughout that summer and became the mecca of enthusiasts and nostalgic romantics from all over Britain. But there was no pleasure to be gained from such a pilgrimage, for the fifty odd engines on shed were all withdrawn, partially dismantled ready for the last journey to the South Wales scrap yards and oblivion. In twos and threes they went, sometimes stealing away by night, as if ashamed to be seen in such a sorry state on the lines where they had so proudly worked.   [N. E. Preedy]

'Z' Class 0-8-0T No.30953 stands between ex-LMS companions outside the shed at Templecombe on 21 April 1956.
Templecombe was one of those communities which was made, and broken, by the railways. Standing at the cross-
roads of the Somerset & Dorset and the LSWR lines, the location grew in importance as a transfer junction and a
large marshalling yard assembled heavy freight trains alongside the SR tracks. Most of the engines at the shed
remained LMS types but the Southern supplied this large shunter for work in the yard.   [Brian Morrison]

Two shots of 'M7' No. 30045 at Seaton on 1 September 1962. The driver has oiled around while the fireman coals up in the most primitive possible manner, slinging the fuel into the bunker with a long-handled shovel. No. 30045 was a regular engine on this branch for a number of years; the branch tank usually spent a week there, returning to Exmouth Junction on Saturday for a weekend boiler washout.

[J. R. Besley]

The long reign of the 'N' Class Moguls in the West Country was drawing to a close when No.31845 was photographed at Okehampton on 27 April 1963. Turntables were symbolic of the steam-age, as the more modern forms of power did not need to turn at the end of a run, but no engineman relished a long run, tender first, with the coal dust blowing back into their faces on an exposed footplate.
[W. L. Underhill]

'Woolworth' No.31875 comes off the table and backs towards Okehampton shed, 1963. This small depot, situated 26 miles west of Exeter, had no regular allocation of its own, but engines from Salisbury, Exeter, Plymouth and Wadebridge called in for servicing. The nearby stone quarries at Meldon gave rise to several turns on heavy ballast trains, for which duties the 'N' Class Moguls were eminently suited.
[R. J. Andrews]

A heavy goods engine of a much earlier era stands outside Okehampton shed on 3 August 1928. No.029 was one of William Adams's standard goods engines, of 1885 vintage, which in the early days of grouping provided power for the stone trains from Meldon.
[H. C. Casserley]

0-6-0T No. DS234 is just visible inside the shed on 18 August 1966. This engine had the distinction of being the only steam locomotive still at work on BR metals west of Exeter at that date.   [John H. Meredith]

ittle depot at Meldon Quarry was not a running shed, but a service shed and its one loco-
e on allocation was not included in the motive power total but as service equipment. For many
, an Adams 0-6-0T shunted in the sidings but powerful USA tank No. DS234 was at work on
ne 1964.   [D. T. Cobbe]

Ivatt tank No. 41322 stands at the water column outside Callington shed. This depot, originally built for the PDSWJR at the end of its nine mile branch from Bere Alston, became a sub-shed of Plymouth Friary, which for many years supplied '02' 0-4-4Ts for the branch passenger trains, but by the 1960's the popular Ivatts had taken over.

[W L. Underhay]

One of the Plymouth squad of 'O2' tanks stands by the coal stage at Friary shed on 10 August 1958. These small tanks, with a few of their larger sisters of the 'M7' Class, were used on local turns on the Southern lines in the Plymouth district, the Turnchapel branch being an 'O2' preserve for many years.   [Brian Morrison]

Friary usually had three or four of the diminutive 'B4' tanks for shunting in the docks around Devonport. They were fitted with spark arrestors, as some of the work was at the timber yards at Oreston. No.30089 looks rather forlorn as it stands in the yard on 10 August 1958, for diesel shunters had arrived in the west to take over the remaining 'B4' turns.

[Brian Morrison]

Ivatt 2-6-2T No.41316 was a new arrival at Friary when seen there on 29 August 1957, for although the shed staff had given the engine a good clean, they had not had time to remove the Ashford (74A) shed plate and substitute the 72D plate which was the code for Friary at the time—later altered to 83H. Friary shed could never compete in prestige with its bigger Western neighbour, Laira, having about twenty engines on strength, including four of the 'West Country' class in the mid-1950's, one of which often worked through to Salisbury with the Plymouth to Brighton train. The shed was quite busy servicing visiting engines which had worked down from Exeter on passenger and freight turns.

[A. R. Butcher]

A pair of men exchange pleasantries with a colleague on Beattie well tank No.30586 as she stands by the coal s at Wadebridge, 11 June 1956. The simple hoist, seen by the stack of coal, was the only mechanical aid for coa available at the depot.

[M. Mens

No. 30585 outside the small two-road shed at Wadebridge, five miles from the terminus of the line at Padstow, was the most westerly shed on the Southern. This wooden structure was built about 1899 when the rails were pushed through to Padstow, but nearby was the old building which had been the engine shed of the Bodmin & Wadebridge railway and, although used as a store until 1968, it is believed that this was the oldest loco shed building surviving in Britain. [P. H. Groom]

'N' Class Mogul No. 31406, of Exmouth Junction, on the turn-table at Wadebridge, 16 May 1963. This table was too small to accommodate the longer Bulleid Pacifics which had to use the one which had been installed at Padstow in 1947. [J. R. Besley]

Wadebridge only had five tanks allocated for its duties, but three of these, the veteran Beattie well tanks dating from 1874/5, were among the most photographed engines in the country. They were usually well-groomed and the crew of No. 30587 giving the little engine a wipe down before the run up the line to Wenford Bridge, the duty which ensured the survival of these Victorian stalwarts. The engine-hoist, used for lifting engines in order to repair hot boxes neatly frames the tank at the east end of the through shed. The offices and stores are visible on the left of the building. [Brian Morris]

A 'Woolworth' at Bude, 7 July 1964. No. 31859 takes 3,500 gallons of water outside the small shed, which was situ[ated] close to the terminus of the branch, 18 miles from Halwill. The engine, shortly about to set off for Exmouth Junc[tion] with the afternoon goods, is carrying an 83D shedplate, the code long associated with Laira, but used by Exm[outh] Junction after the boundary reorganisation of 1963.

[D. T. Co[bbe]

The North Cornwall line never seemed quite the same after 1962 when the famous 'T9s' finally disappeared from service. At least one of these 'Greyhounds' was stabled at Wadebridge overnight, while another invariably worked down with the 9.56 a.m. from Okehampton. No. 30718 is coming off the shed to work a local down to Padstow on 2 August 1960.

[D. T. Cobbe]

Bude depot usually stabled a tank from Exmouth Junction for the local turns to Halwill. As with other West Country branches, 'M7s' provided the power for many years, but late in 1962 the large free-running Standard Class '4' 2-6-4Ts came to Exmouth Junction and were used very successfully on this branch. Three pairs of locomen were based at the depot, which became dieselised in 1965 and closed, with the line, in October 1966.

[J. R. Besley]

Two of the Isle of Wight's 'O2' tanks, No.31 *Chale* and No.21 *Sandown*, at the back of Ryde shed on 20 July 1963. Typical of most locomotive sheds were the pits between the rails to facilitate access to the underside of engines, and smoke ducts under the roof to take away smoke and steam to the outside atmosphere. The scene also shows the usual paraphernalia of a shed, including the simple tools at the bench, washout hoses and the cycles of the shed staff.

[D. M. Cox]

close up at Bude shows No.31845 emerging, with steam up, from the shed. In common with most small sub-sheds, coaling arrangements were crude, the fuel being hand-loaded from the stack situated on a raised platform ngside the track. The quality of the coal was of great concern to the footplatemen; at least this stack has some od sized lumps amongst the slack and dust.

[W. L. Underhay]

The majority of the Isle of Wight locomotives were '02s'; a selection of the class is on view at Ryde on 28 August 1965.
[M. J. Messenger]

No. 33 *Bembridge* takes water outside the shed. These small tanks had a capacity of 800 gallons and needed frequent replenishment during a spell of duty away from the shed.
[M. J. Messenger]

No. 18 *Ningwood* and No. 30 *Shorwell* bask in the summer sunshine at Ryde, 29 August 1965.
[M. J. Messenger]

:hools' 4-4-0 No.30916 *Whitgift* on shed at Bricklayers Arms, situated off the Old Kent Road. These handsome
ee-cylinder engines were superb performers on Eastern Section lines from 1930 until the end of steam working in
1. This particular engine has come up to Town from Ramsgate, but Bricklayers Arms usually numbered a dozen
these magnificent Maunsells on its books for working express turns from Charing Cross down to the Kent coast.

[N. E. Preedy]

Bulleid Pacifics up from the coast called in for servicing at the London end of their express duties. Bricklayers Arms
was a rambling depot with a number of separate shed buildings and a large repair shop. At times its allocation topped
the 100-engine mark, with a wide cross-section of types, ranging from 'Schools' and 'King Arthurs' for the heaviest
turns, through a large number of smaller 4-4-0s for secondary passenger work, to a host of 2-6-0s and 0-6-0s for the
considerable number of freight turns rostered to the shed.

[D. T. Cobbe]

Maunsell mixed-traffics outside the shed in April 1949. No. 31826 was one of four 'N' Class 2-6-0s shedded, with a pair of 'U1s', at Bricklayers Arms at that time. By 1953 there were seventeen Moguls at the depot, the newcomers having replaced retired 0-6-0s.

[Peter Winding]

Outside Ryde shed; above, No. 19 *Osborne* seen in October 1951 and below, No. 29 *Alverstone* in the summer of 1965. The design of the '02s' originated with Adams on the South Western in 1889 and, following the Grouping of 1923, 21 of the class (Nos. 14–34) were shipped across to the Isle of Wight, having been modified by the addition of Westinghouse air-brake equipment and enlarged coal bunkers. Two more (Nos. 35 & 36) followed in April 1949.

[T. P. Cooper]

e faithful Wainwright 'C' Class
-0s were active at Bricklayers Arms
til the end of steam working in the
uth East. Nos. 31694 and 31293 are
en outside the shed on 11 March
51. [D. T. Cobbe]

The shed yard at Ashford, 10 September 1960. The variety of engines, ranging from pre-Grouping 'C' 0-6-0s, through the Maunsell Moguls and 4-4-0s to post-war Bulleid and Standard classes, was typical of the locomotives to be seen at this District Headquarters. [D. T. Cobbe]

No. 31489, one of Maunsell's 'D1' rebuilds, stands between a pair of post-war tanks at Ashford, 14 April 1958. Eastern Section crews performed wonders with these moderately sized engines, which had modern long-travel piston valves and high superheat, making them strong pullers and extremely free-running on favourable gradients. [A. R. Butcher]

Ashford shed had been associated with 'King Arthurs' for many years, usually having four or five of the six-wheeled-tender variety on allocation. Therefore it was appropriate that an 'Arthur' should take part in a final steam tour of Kent on 25 February 1962, although No. 30782 *Sir Brian* was a stranger to the area, having spent years at Nine Elms and Bournemouth (71B) sheds. Its companion is 'Schools' No. 30926 *Repton* and both engines make a fine sight with steam up and the winter sun shining on their gleaming paintwork.   [A. R. Butcher]

With the Works close at hand, it was not surprising to see freshly repainted engines on shed at Ashford. 'C2X' 0-6-0 No.32441 looks neat and tidy between a 4-4-0 and a 'Q1' 0-6-0, 24 September 1955.

[Brian Morrison]

Three locomotive generations outside Ashford shed on 14 April 1958; pre-Grouping 'C' 0-6-0 No.31271 contrasts with a Southern Railway 'King Arthur' and BR Standard 4-6-0 No.75068.

[A. R. Butcher]

'Schools' No. 30938 *St. Olave's* is prepared for the road at Ashford on 24 September 1955. The work of preparation was an important, though onerous, daily chore. The driver is seen oiling the motion, the time for which task varied from class to class, but averaged about an hour. Three-cylinder locomotives were not popular in this respect, as access to the inside set of Walschaerts valve gear was often difficult, especially for older and stouter drivers! But should this work be skimped, the bearings would soon overheat when the engine was at work. The fireman has the blower on, building up a good hot fire and the coal is stacked well forward on the tender. Often crews prepared the engine before their trip, but on some rosters the work would be performed by men on 'Preparation and Disposal' duties at the shed. [Brian Morrison]

With cotton waste in hand, the driver of 'Schools' No. 30918 *Hurstpierpoint* has a final round of inspection before going off Dover shed. This engine, along with sister No. 30930 *Radley*, has been fitted with a Lemaitre blast pipe and large diameter chimney, but these modifications did not improve the performance to any great extent, so only 21 out of 40 members of the class were modified.

[N. E. Preedy]

'Battle of Britain' Pacific No. 34088 *213 Squadron* has crept on to the table at Dover to turn after its run down from Victoria on the 'Golden Arrow' Pullman boat train. This was one of the major prestige trains of the Southern and Stewarts Lane shed always turned out an immaculate engine for the job. No. 34088 is no exception. Even the copper pipes to the injectors have been scoured and the whole engine provides a good, if not typical, advertisement for British locomotives at that time (25 July 1960). [D. T. Cobbe]

144-ton 'Merchant Navy'
Pacific No. 35029
Ellerman Lines swings
round on the vacuum
operated turntable at
Dover, 20 June 1953. At
this date, this engine and
No. 35030 were allocated
to Dover shed for
working the heaviest
boat trains to Victoria.

[J. R. Besley]

Class No.31113 has
[be]en fully coaled at the
[D]over stage, and awaits
[its] turn of duty in the
[sh]ed yard. The depot had
[an] allocation of over
[fif]ty locomotives during
[th]e 1950's, including a
[co]nsiderable number of
[pa]ssenger engines for
[th]e services to London.
[Peter Winding]

No.31174, one of a pair of Stirling 'R1' 0-6-0 tanks, berthed by the turntable at Folkestone Junction
shed in April 1959. This small depot was a sub-shed of Dover and had seven tanks allocated in the
late 1950's.   [Peter Winding]

Diminutive 'P' Class 0-6-0 No.31323 looks tiny alongside one of Dover's 'King Arthurs' outside the
shed, April 1959.   [Peter Winding]

[A] pair of 'WD' 2-8-0s,
[N]os.79199 and 78597, at
[D]over in April 1949.
[T]hese wartime 'Austerity'
[en]gines were built to the
[d]esign of R. A. Riddles
[fo]r the Ministry of
[S]upply and worked
[th]roughout Britain as
[w]ell as in many parts of
[E]urope. The Southern
[h]ad some at Feltham and
[B]ricklayers Arms, but by
[19]53 all had left the
[R]egion. [Peter Winding]

Stirling 'R1' 0-6-0Ts stand idle and neglected outside Folkestone Junction shed in April 1959. The cause for this can just be discerned in the gloomy interior of the shed—ex-GWR pannier tanks which had recently arrived to take over the 'R1' duties at Folkestone Harbour. For many years the old tanks had lifted boat trains up the incline from the Harbour to the Junction, three being required for the heaviest trains.   [Peter Winding]

Three of the newcomers at Folkestone Junction—No. 4631, with Nos. 4626 and 4601 inside the shed. [Peter Winding]

y engines among the smoke and steam of Dover shed yard in April 1959. No.31757, of Ashford, was one of the
ul Maunsell 'L1' 4-4-0s introduced by Richard Maunsell in 1926 for secondary passenger duties on the Eastern
tion routes. The modern Standard, No.75066, would also take its turn working lighter trains up to London.
[Peter Winding]

'L' Class 4-4-0 No.31760, of Nine Elms, borrowed by the Eastern Section for a run to Dover, is seen on the pits, 3 June
1961. The wagons on the steep incline have been pushed up by the shed pilot and the coal which they contain will be
emptied on to the coal stage for loading on to the locomotives.
[D. T. Cobbe]

St. Leonards shed in July 1961. By this date there was little steam working in the area, hence the solitary Mogul on view. In the background is St. Leonards (West Marina) station.   [A. R. Butcher]

In Southern Days the shed yard was much more crowded, as this selection of 4-4-0s and 0-6-0s proves.
[Lens of Sutton]

An 'H1' tank and a brace of 'Schools' outside the shed in BR days.
[Lens of Sutton]

'D3' 0-4-4T No.32385, of Eastbourne (75G) shed, outside St. Leonards on 3 December 1952. The small tank is undergoing repairs, as both cylinder heads can be seen resting in the running plates beneath the smokebox. There is also a view of the splendid nameplate on No.30910 *Merchant Taylors*, one of the St. Leonards stud of 'Schools' Class 4-4-0s. [J. R. Besley]

A little later in the day No. 30910 *Merchant Taylors* comes off the Loco for a run up to London Bridge via the Quarry Line, the route for which the class was specifically designed. Because of the very restricted loading gauge on that line, the cab profile of these fine 4-4-0s was sloped to allow a safe passage through the narrow tunnels. St. Leonards had Nos. 30900–30910 for about 25 years and looked after them with loving care.

[J. R. Besley]

Norwood Junction shed in the mid-1930's with a 'C2X' 0-6-0 simmering in the foreground. The steep incline leading up to the coalstage is most noticeable in this view. [Lens of Sutton]

Years later, in September 1959, a 'C2X' still forms the centrepiece of a view at Norwood Junction. The fireman is clambering on to the footplate as his driver glances around before leaving the depot. On the same line can be seen the bunker of one of the four powerful 'W' Class 2-6-4 tanks which were used by the shed for inter-Regional transfer freights in the London area. [N. E. Preedy]

Seen on 3 June 1956, 'Q' Class 0-6-0 No. 30549, shedded at Norwood Junction (75C), differed from the other 'Qs' in that it had a stovepipe chimney, a feature which added little to the engine's appearance or its steaming ability.　　　[A. R. Carpenter]

Numerous freights from other Regions crossed London to be sorted in the marshalling yard near the shed. Stanier '8F' 2-8-0 No. 48074 of Willesden (1A) shed eases a heavy load down the bank past the shed yard.　　　[Lens of Sutton]

Maunsell engines at the Redhill coal stage in July 1964. Redhill engines and men worked on the busy cross-cc route between Reading and the South coast, and for these turns used such moderate sized power as 'Q' 0-6-0 No.30543 and 'U' Class Mogul No.31790. The largest locomotives that had been allocated to the depot the six-wheeled tender 'S15' 4-6-0s, but these had all been moved away to Feltham by this time. [G. D.

Redhill (75B) shed was tucked into the fork between the Tonbridge and Brighton lines south of the station. This 1964 panorama reveals a number of Maunsell engines still active among the Standards of more recent vintage. Of even greater interest is the presence of Eastern Region 'B1' 4-6-0 No.61313, of Canklow (41D), shed. This had probably worked south with an excursion train from the North of England via the Western Region at Reading and had called at the shed for attention. Note the three snow ploughs which will not be needed on this fine summer day.

[G. D. King]

A view, taken from the turntable, showing an assortment of Maunsell locomotives in the shed yard at Redhill on 6 March 1961. 'Schools' 4-4-0s Nos. 30914 *Eastbourne* and 30909 *St. Paul's* have been transferred to the Reading–Redhill services following the electrification schemes in Kent, while the 'U' Class Moguls are old stagers in the area. Unfortunately, the big 4-4-0s were past their prime and rather neglected, a sad end to a glorious career.

[A. R. Butcher]

411, one of the left-hand-batch of 'N' Class Moguls s on to Redhill table in the ner of 1964.   [G. D. King]

e a mixture at Redhill on a mer evening in 1964. dard Class '5' 4-6-0 No. 2 is from the LMR, with B1' 4-6-0 No.61313 seen in npany with Standard Class -6-4T No.80152 and an 'N' ss 2-6-0 of Southern way vintage.   [G. D. King]

Engine turning was made much easier with the introduction of vacuum-operated motors for the turntables. Manually operated tables were difficult to rotate, especially if the engines were not centred correctly, but the fireman of No.31831 can have a ride as the Mogul, using its ejector to actuate the motor, revolves at Redhill on 3 January 1965.   [G. D. King]

Victorian cleanliness of engines and shed premises in 'the good old days' at Tunbridge Wells (West). Such a s
reveals the sad deterioration which took place over the years in steam railway working conditions, but the new d
and electric depots are clean workshops in the old tradition. Railway lore has it that the nineteenth century fore
always tested the quality of cleaning on the locomotives by running his white handkerchief over the paintwork. T
LBSCR engines would surely have passed even that stringent test!   [Lens of Su

Standard Class '3' 2-6-2T No.82024, complete with an old Exmouth Junction (72A) shedplate, on the pits at Redhill,
January 1965. The engine appears to be leaking steam from every possible joint and gland; such was the machinery
with which the locomen had to work on many lines in the final days of steam.   [G. D. King]

Although 'push and pull' 'H' Class 0-4-4T No.31521 cannot match the sparkling condition of its forebears above, considerable care has obviously been taken by the crew to stack sufficient coal on the bunker of the little tank for the day's work from Tunbridge Wells (West), 26 January 1961. [J. R. Besley]

Standard Class '4' 2-6-4T No. 80033 at rest inside Tunbridge Wells (West) shed in January 1961. Behind the locomotive is the notice boar a very important feature in every running shed. Drivers were allowed time to 'read th notices', some of which were of vital importance, such as temporary speed restrictions and other abnormal conditio to be encountered en route. The duty roster for the enginemen's Links would be posted daily, amongst a grea deal of other general information.   [J. R. Besle

The Standards operated from Tunbridge Wells (West) she for several years, some worki the Oxted line traffic which were among the last steam-hauled trains to be seen on t Central Section lines out of Victoria. No. 80064 is seen on 23 December 1961.

[A. R. Butch

New Cross Gate shed was an LBSCR stronghold in East London—a large depot, consisting of several sheds and repair shops, situated close to the station of the same name on the line from London Bridge. No. 2038 *Portland Bill*, one of Douglas Earle Marsh's 'H1' Atlantics of 1905 is seen, with a variety ot Moguls, in the shed yard in September 1946. Below, a month or so earlier is 'E4' 0-6-2T No. 2468 posed by the sand furnace. Sand was a vital commodity for steam engines, but had to be thoroughly dry, otherwise it would not run freely down to the rails and alleviate slipping. It was the fireman's task to collect a sufficient amount from the furnace before a trip and fill up the sand boxes on his engine.

[Peter Winding]

'U1' 2-6-0 No.31891, in early British Railways livery, outside the shed at New Cross Gate in 1948. The shed's allocation (36 engines) was transferred early in 1947 and the duties were acquired by Bricklayers Arms and Norwood Junction, although the shed was retained as a stabling point and repair depot until the autumn of 1951.

[Peter Winding]

'I1X' 4-4-2 No.2006 under repair outside New Cross Gate shed in August 1946. The shed's imminent decline in status is foreshadowed by the deteriorating state of the building.

[Peter Winding]